# WHEN WE WERE BIRDS

Miller Williams Poetry Series
EDITED BY BILLY COLLINS

# WHEN WE WERE BIRDS

*Poems by Joe Wilkins*

The University of Arkansas Press

FAYETTEVILLE

2016

ISBN: 978-1-55728-697-0

e-ISBN: 978-1-61075-583-2

20   19   18   17   16      5   4   3   2   1

Text design by Ellen Beeler

♾ The paper used in this publication meets the minimum requirements of the American National Standard for Permanence of Paper for Printed Library Materials Z39.48-1984.

Library of Congress Control Number: 2015952238

*For Liz, Walter, and Edie—*
*these fugitive hearts.*

*Yes, we were trembling.*
*We have not stopped trembling yet.*

—James Baldwin

# SERIES EDITOR'S PREFACE

When the University of Arkansas Press asked if I would act as editor for the coming year's annual poetry prize named in honor of Miller Williams, the press's cofounder, long-time director, and progenitor of its poetry program, I was quick to accept. Since 1988 when he published my first full-length book, *The Apple That Astonished Paris*, I have felt indebted to Miller, who died in January 2015 at the age of eighty-four.

When he first spotted my poetry, I was forty-six years old with two chapbooks only. Not a pretty sight.

I have him to thank for first carrying me across that critical line dividing *no book* from *book*, thus turning me, at last, into a "published poet." I was especially eager to take on this task because it is a publication prize that may bring to light other first books. In fact, from the beginning of his time at the press, it was Miller's practice to publish one poet's first book every year. Then in 1990 this commitment was formalized when Miller awarded the first Arkansas Poetry Prize. Fittingly, it was renamed the Miller Williams Poetry Prize after his retirement and has grown to welcome work from both published and unpublished writers alike.

Miller Williams was more than my first editor. Over the years, he and I became friends, but even more importantly, before my involvement with the press, he served as a kind of literary father to me as his own straightforward, sometimes folksy, sometimes witty, and always trenchant poems became to me models of how poems could sound and how they could go. He was one of the poets who showed me that humor could be a legitimate mode in poetry—that a poem could be humorous without being silly or merely comical. He also showed me that a plain-spoken poem did not have to be imaginatively plain. Younger poets today could learn much from his example, as I did.

Given his extensive and distinguished career, it's surprising that Miller hasn't enjoyed a more prominent position on the American literary map. As his daughter became well known as a singer and recording artist, Miller became known to many as the father of Lucinda Williams. Miller and Lucinda even appeared on stage together several times performing a father-daughter act of song and poetry. And Miller enjoyed a bright, shining moment when Bill Clinton chose him to be the inaugural poet at his second inauguration in 1997. The poem he wrote for that day, "Of History and Hope," is a meditation on how "we have memorized America." In turning to the children of our country he broadens a nursery rhyme question by asking "How does our garden grow?" Occasional poems, especially for occasions of such importance, are notoriously difficult—some would say impossible—to write with success. But Miller rose to this lofty occasion and produced a winner. His confident reading of the poem before the nation added cultural and emotional weight to the morning's ceremony.

Apart from such public recognitions, most would agree that Miller's fuller legacy lies in his teaching and publishing career, which covered four decades. In that time, he published over a dozen books of his own poetry and literary theory. His accomplishments as a writing poet and working editor are what will speak for Miller in the years to come. The qualities of his poems make them immediately likeable and pleasurable. They sound as if they were spoken, not just written, and they show a courteous, engaging awareness of the presence of a reader. Miller knew that the idea behind a good poem is to make the reader feel something, rather than to merely display the poet's emotional state, which usually boils down to some form of misery. Miller also possessed the authority of experience to produce poems that were just plain wise.

With these attributes in mind, I began the judging of this year's prize. On the lookout for poems that Miller would approve of, that is, poems that seemed to be consciously or unconsciously in the Miller Williams School, I read and read. But in reading these scores of manuscripts, I realized that applying such narrow criteria would be selling Miller short. His tastes in poetry were clearly broader than the stylistic territory of his own verse; he published poets as different from one another as John Ciardi and Jimmy Carter. I readjusted and began to look for poems I thought Miller would delight in reading, instead of echoes of his own poems. This took some second-guessing, but I'm confident that Miller would enthusiastically approve of this year's selections.

Broadening the field of judgment brought happy results. The work of four very different poets, who have readability, freshness of language, and seriousness of intent in common, stood out among the stack of submissions.

Andrew Gent's [explicit lyrics] is a fascinating collection of poems that slip through their own cracks and seem to vanish before the reader's eyes. Influences are a matter of guesswork, but I'd say he has learned some of his admirable tricks from Yannis Ritsos and some of the New York School. Surprises lurk on almost every page. See You Soon, the casual title of Laura McKee's book, contains poems of powerful feeling that seem composed in the kind of tranquility of recollection, which Wordsworth recommended. Living in a country that appears to be continually involved in war on many fronts, readers will find in Brock Jones's Cenotaph a new way of thinking and feeling about the realities of combat. It is difficult to write war poetry because the subject is pre-loaded with emotional weight, but Jones more than manages to render precisely the mess of war with tenderness and insight. Joe Wilkins's poems are located in the tradition of the sacred, but holiness here is found in common experience. When We Were Birds, as the title indicates, is full of imaginative novelty as well as reminders that miraculous secrets are hidden in the fabric of everyday life.

In short we have here a gathering of young poets whose work, I think, would have fully engaged and gladdened Miller Williams. Because I have sat with him there, I can picture Miller in his study turning the pages, maybe stopping to make a pencil note in a margin. Miller's wider hope, of course, was that the poems published in this series would find a broad readership, ready to be delighted and inspired. I join my old friend and editor in that wish.

—Billy Collins

# ACKNOWLEDGMENTS

Thanks to the editors of the following magazines, where versions of these poems first appeared:

*Alaska Quarterly Review*: "The Day We Finish Painting the Bedroom, My Wife's Father E-mails Us His Suicide Note"

*Beloit Poetry Journal*: "Note to My Unborn Son concerning Quickening"

*Blackbird*: "Wish"

*Coachella Review*: "Ragged Point Road (Why in the night do boys)"

*Codex*: "Arguing with James Baldwin the Day after the Reelection of Barack Obama"

*Conte*: "Colic"

*Contrary*: "The Garage Sale Daze Meditations"

*Dialogist*: "Note to My Unborn Son concerning Time, Fear, and Impending Fatherhood"; "Today, the Neighbor Girl Wore a Blue Dress, and Her Doll Was Naughty at Tea"

*Harpur Palate*: "An Ode for Leaving the Place You Call Home"; "Like Bread the Light"

*Hawk & Handsaw*: "Missouri River"

*International Journal of Servant Leadership*: "The Can Picker, 1st & Cowls"; "Me & Mississippi"

*iO Poetry*: "Note to My Unborn Son concerning Canadian Folk Music"

*Linebreak*: "Absence"; "Encomium, Driving Highway 49 South"; "Leviathan"

*Mayday*: "Each Word Holds the World"; "Six Days' Lament"

*The Michigan Quarterly Review*: "Eight Letters of Explanation, Acknowledgment, & Apology on the Occasion of My Son's First Birthday"

*Mid-American Review*: "Anyone who has eyes for seeing should see"

*The Minnesota Review*: "Caddo River Elegy"

*The Nashville Review*: "A Story We Might Follow"; "Ragged Point Road (Some twenty miles out)"

*Nimrod*: "'Where Was I before I Was Born?'"

*North American Review*: "Complaint with Parking Lot Vegetable Stand & Child's Cry"

*Orion*: "Drought"

*Poetry Northwest*: "Poem thinning out into prayer"

*The Puritan*: "Complaint with the Turning of the Seasons & Shined Shoes"

*Redactions*: "Note to My Unborn Son concerning Manufacturing Economics and Courage"

*River Styx*: "Prairie Race Relations, Lodge Grass, One Sunday Afternoon"

*The San Pedro River Review*: "Note to My Unborn Son concerning the Second Law of Thermodynamics"; "The Spirit Entering as Midnight Wind"

*Shaking*: "Note to My Unborn Son concerning the Peculiarities of Faith"

*Slate*: "The Gospel according to Kelly, Night Shift Manager, Forest City Fuel & Foods"

*The Southern Review*: "J&W Redemption, Highway 9, North Iowa"; "My Son Asks for the Story about When We Were Birds"

*The Southern Poetry Review*: "Fishcutter"

*Tahoma Literary Review*: "Littlelight"

*Talking River*: "Complaint with Exhaustion & Amateur Theology"; "With the Kisses of Many"

*Terrain*: "Complaint with Drought and Economic Downturn"

*Tupelo Quarterly*: "Eat Stone and Go On"

"Eat Stone and Go On" was reprinted in *FEAST: Poetry and Recipes for a Full Seating at Dinner* (Black Lawrence Press 2015). "Note to My Unborn Son concerning Our First Birthing Class" first appeared in *Two Weeks: A Digital Anthology of Contemporary Poetry* (Linebreak Press 2011). A number of these poems also appeared in the limited-edition chapbook *Leviathan* (*Iron Horse* 16.5).

Thanks to Linfield College for the time, space, and challenge to write. Thanks as well to the Sustainable Arts Foundation for a Promise Award and to the Margery Davis Boyden Wilderness Writing Residency for, among other things, the view of Rattlesnake Ridge.

And a special thanks to Steve Coughlin, Lucas Howell, Shann Ray, Lex Runciman, and Robert Wrigley for their time and attention to these poems.

# CONTENTS

# III

# IV

# V

WHEN WE WERE BIRDS

## My Son Asks for the Story about When We Were Birds

When we were birds,
we veered & wheeled, we flapped & looped—

it's true, we flew. When we were birds,
we dined on tiny silver fish
& the watery hearts
of flowers. When we were birds,

we sistered the dragonfly,
brothered the night-wise bat,

& sometimes when we were birds,

we rose as high as we could go—
light cold & strange—

& when we opened our beaked mouths,
sundown poured like wine
down our throats.

When we were birds,
we worshipped trees, rivers, mountains,

sage knots, rain, gizzard rocks, grub-shot dung piles,

& like all good beasts & wise green things,

the mothering sun. We had many gods
when we were birds,

& each in her own way
was good to us, even winter fog,

which found us huddling
in salal or silk tassel,
singing low, sweet songs & closing
our blood-rich eyes & sleeping
the troubled sleep of birds. Yes,

even when we were birds,
we were sometimes troubled & tired,

sad for no reason,

& so pretended we were not birds
& fell like stones—

the earth hurtling up to meet us,
our trussed bones readying
to be shattered, our unusually large hearts
pounding for nothing—

yet at the last minute we would flap
& lift & as we flew shudderingly away,

we told ourselves that this falling—

we would remember. We thought

we would always
be birds. We didn't know.

We didn't know
we could love one another

with such ferocity. That we should.

I

# Eat Stone and Go On

*Isn't it a shame*, my grandmother said,
silver fork in her shivering fist,

*how we have to go on eating?*
We were sitting up to burnt chuck,

potatoes in their dirty jackets,
and hunks of Irish brown bread,

the two of us sitting up at the old wood table,
the one years ago my grandfather built

of planks pulled from an abandoned mine.
My grandmother stared at her plate.

She couldn't have been
more than a hundred pounds then,

the palsy at work in her hands,
her hung face. I was fifteen and hungry.

I had shoveled for her that day
two tons of furnace coal.

It was nearly winter. The summer past,
my grandfather had gone ahead

and died. Even if it was only
soda bread and fried steaks, I see now

it was something. I shoveled
another forkful of buttered potato

into my mouth, bits of the stone
we call salt between my teeth.

# Note to My Unborn Son concerning Quickening

The wind this morning,
like a meanness in the world,

spit snow thick and drifted—
but right at noon

that runaway sky
went silver-blue, bright

and disquieting as the coins
of some far country.

# Ragged Point Road

Some twenty miles out this road gives way to grass.
I stopped there once, no track for miles
but mine,

and that one already
springing back, the grass erasing
my passage. I wasn't much more than a boy—

the blown dust a fist against my face, my father
dead the February before,
and ever since

my mother silent and moon-faced at the kitchen table,
her hand around a cup
of coffee, cold.

For chokecherries
I had an old ice-cream bucket,
deer-hide gloves for the lambs' blood stain of them

on my fingers. I knew I was on my own, didn't believe
in anything but my few years
of dry seasons—

though what a winter it had been. Snow
high as me, and higher. Even these bone-scape plains
erased, gone,

and gone too
the shelterbelt, corrals, broken-
backed sheep shed my father let lean and, in his sickness,

fall. That day,
I didn't know that so long as the river swells
with what the mountains give, chokecherries bloom

and bloom and never
berry. I wandered the bank. I'd never seen
the river so full, would never

see it so full again. And not a chokecherry to be found—
the trees a mess of wasp-happy
blossoms.

# An Ode for Leaving the Place You Call Home

I scramble down the weedy bank,
crawl across the rocks, sit on my heels
beneath the bridge.

Everything is mud and rust,
and Charles + Katie = Forever.

The river, of course, is quick, deep,
a great dark thing refusing to be ignored—
the flood line runs up the iron the height of a man.

       *

Now the sky blazes
above mile after mile of cornfield,
slough, gravel road, and those always
white two-story farmhouses—
and the grown son slings hay to the goats,
and the old father curses the tractor.

*Look, here is the world!*
*The world of light that lives between darkness*
*and darkness! Here is the world!* the herons cry,
those river lovers, those iridescent brothers
of sun and moon, white winged
pilgrims who make their home
wherever silver fish rise for nymphs—

and now the son looks up,
and the father,

14

and here they are,
two men grown like corn from the dark
earth of the Middle West, staring at the bird-shot sky.

*

This is the poem I'd show you,
if you were alive.

But you've been gone
these twenty years. And I'm living

in this land without mountains,
without pines, this place

of slow waters and hogs,
the late summer leaves of corn—

I guess you wouldn't like it.
At least that's what I tell myself,

hunkered up beneath the bridge,
my chin on my knees.

I don't really know.
I've long forgotten every moment

we ever shared. There's nothing
to be done for it, really—

my breath already
so much dust.

*

Now the sun is gone.
Now the aluminum plant clangs
with shift change—

across the gravel road, a hulking man
in blue jeans and suspenders, and that's it,
stands in his doorway, sucks on a cigarette.

He stares into the lights of the flatbed trucks
and beat-up Buicks streaming out the lot toward town,
his white belly curving like the earth curves, dark seas
of hair at his nipples. He shivers. Says, *Hurry now,
Bitsy. Hurry!* to the small dog

shitting in the rhododendrons.
And turning from it all, a boy runs across
the train tracks, sidesteps through the pokeweed

and silver cans littering the ditch bank.
*This is my world,* he thinks, *pokeweed,
gravel road, that man*

*without a shirt saying Bitsy.*
The boy realizes he is not happy about this,
he wonders if he should do something. But what?
What can he do about the way smoke leaks
from that man's lips?

What can he do about weeds cracking
like bones beneath his steps?
He doesn't know—

he jams his fists in his pockets,
hunches his shoulders against the wind. Above him,
a wash of herons darkens the moon's pocked face.

   *

What can I say?

I am sure only of highways and dust,
afternoon cigarettes,

thunderstorms, the dark night shot with stars,
the sadness of white houses in the dark.

Tell me, what should I do?

Here I am in the Middle West,
a thousand miles from my father's grave—

I still dream Montana. I still believe
for each of us there is a country

we call home—

where the river rises
and the moon burns its white hole in the sky

and, like prayers, the herons swing
between wind and water,

where the son sometimes turns away

from the father, where we die
but die home.

# Leviathan

*An inmate at the Winnebago County Jail escaped for a number of hours before north Iowa authorities captured him.*
—KTTC, NBC affiliate, February 12, 2010

*When I lie down, I say, When shall I arise, and the night be gone?*
—Job, 7:4

There was a time along the river,
                 in the snow and cold. I didn't know
where I was going. I had come crashing
through river birch, willows,
                 sumac that tore my feet.
I had no shoes. My pants were a problem. Baggy, striped.
I took them off. Everything,
                 I took it off. There
along the frozen river I stripped bare-ass naked—
fat carp were iced into the falls, some big dark owl came over
quiet as suffering Christ,
                 and I was my body,
like a boy out all day and who cares how cold it is.
My breaths steamed out in chuffs and huffs,
my tongue tasted weeds and water,
                 black leach-track stones
up from the river's muddy bottom. Beneath the ice,
even there, the river knows. So I followed.
Wherever it was going.
                 Red flags trailing from my blue feet.

Out the country club's picture window, I guess, someone
saw me. Or my bleeding.
       And now I sit here warm as toast,
my body lost, toeless feet black as stones.
Why? What's it worth?
                       I tell you every night
I dream the Winnebago River, long wing of ice
and leaning, penitent trees. Miracle carp
                         unfroze, flopping
bare-assed in the snow. Sirens. And this time I stop,
still as river birch: Above me my owl god
of flight and silence,
                   and having with my own eyes seen,
I am Job. The falling snow? Not silver coins or rings,
not some thousand-thousand sheep.
       For as they rush out—
rifles, bullhorns, blackshoes, blackshoes—
my rucked and filthy skin
       carries this light-shot skin of snow.

## The Day We Finish Painting the Bedroom, My Wife's Father E-mails Us His Suicide Note

The west wall,
back of the headboard,

is *Tuscan Hillside.*
The rest: *Aged Olive.*

It looks nice. Better,
I think, than the wine

and pale salmon
of the couple

before us. The realtor
mentioned they

were "a good
Christian family," so

as we painted,
we played at divining

from each choice
something

of their lives: What
does such a dark red say

about eschatology?
Maybe fishbelly

has something to do
with forgiveness?

And did he weep
only that once

when the traveling choir,
robed in resplendent

vermilion, went silent?
Did she, despite his protests

and in front of the deacon,
put her mouth to his ear

and whisper?
Did they argue?

Did they hide inside
silence? Did they even

know each other?
It was fun, while

it lasted. But now,
brushes drying,

dropcloth rolled away,
we're left with our own

strange greens.

## Note to My Son concerning Our First Birthing Class

Last night the nurse—
rail thin and, by half, too happy—
clicked a picture onto the screen. *Cervix,*

she announced. Then clicked, and clicked again:
*Heavy spotting. Mucus plug. Anal pile. Now,*
*introduce your partner!*

So, your mother gave my name. Others
hit that *husband* hard. Some few mumbled only,
*friend.* Like up front

the heavy-chested girl
in the high-school basketball jacket—
the big boy beside her,

with his shaved head and narrow strap of beard,
shrinking in his seat. When in the dark
the burst of blood became

a puckered child,
he was close to crying. He blinked
and blinked, worked at his eyes

with the backs of his hands,
as if his hands—
hands that palm the ball, that eat the very air,

that slide so easily up the ivory
of her thighs—here, too, knew what to do:
just block out the light.

# Complaint with the Turning of the Season & Shined Shoes

come an early summer evening    that breeze in the daisies
they walk    arrhythmic    off kilter    thin-necked daisies

foundering in the wind    touch only now & then
& just their mottled hands    they must each

be nearly ninety    like an old coat the left half of her
hung    his fly undone    I guess they get along    but why

why all winter I swaddled that rose in burlap & anyway
it up & died    why when I'm not looking cat snaps

the lazy necks of fledglings    why the blueing daisies
the falling tree flowers    his shined shoes    why at the corner

why that's where I looked    why in the slip & tremble
of her two hands she took once more & touched his face

# Drought

Cowlicked, freckled, skinny as a barn cat—
she had me on my back,

was pulling me right out of my blue jeans.
It was late summer, at least,

and the river had the clean stink of gravel—
no rotting tires or mud-foundered bullhead—

a warm wind silvered
the leaves of cottonwoods,

the crows making a racket
in the stripped chokecherries like it might

even matter.
Maybe it does matter—

the grass itched my bare ass, her thighs
pearled as river shells.

# The Gospel according to Kelly, Night Shift Manager, Forest City Fuel & Foods

*What sells in a recession: canned goods and condoms. Wine and liquor were also up.*

—Time Magazine

*Blessed are those who hunger and thirst . . . they shall have their fill.*

—Matthew, 5:6

When you come, with your hunger, I will fill you—
tier upon tier of bubble gum & breath mints & sour balls,

stacks of weeks-old white bread, slick packages of bologna,
sweet pickles & okra pickles & the pickled underlips of pigs,

all manner of potted meats & yellowed salad dressing & the hen
long ago unhinged & shellacked & frozen & just this morning

tossed & fried in a goodly amount of brown grease
& all these hours later deepening in flavor & tang

beneath the buttery light of a heat lamp for you, for you.
When you come, with your thirst, I will slake you—

in cloudy plastic bottles the generic blue juice that stains
alike the round mouths of babes & derelicts, the tall cans

of caffeinated syrup sucked down by bony, acned boys,
whose necks hitch & chuckle & shake, who wipe wet mouths

on shirtsleeves, who pay with bills rumpled in warm palms
& stink of river mud & yeast, who in a few short years will rise

& in dark fits of themselves wander the wine aisle
& pour down those same hitching throats squat bottles

of Mad Dog, & so, those Friday evenings, when boys wander
& itch & lick their chapped lips, they will find chocolate milk

is on sale, & Gatorade, & Mountain Dew, & the strange
electric blue juice they drank when they were not boys

but boys, & for you, all of this is for you. When you come,
the teeth of late winter gnashing at your fat heart's flesh—

I will pile high & higher the boxes of chocolate donuts,
deftly heft the half-rack of High Life, the Bic & cigarettes,

& turn, as you ask me to turn, & unlock the glass case,
for I do not understand but understand this night you need

a jackknife, a box of condoms, NoDoz, NyQuil—I will,
& without slinging a single word, ring up each item

& place each in a small, white sack & bless & bless
these hungers, these throat-wracking thirsts—like hope

they are what we have, & here in the far corner of the night,
among the bean-rusted fields & gutted factories of the Midwest—

what else do we have? Stranger, a scuff of light shatters
the linoleum. Let me lay my hand a moment in yours,
count out for you these few coins.

# II

# Note to My Unborn Son concerning Manufacturing Economics and Courage

Oh, now they have closed the factory.
We do not work at the factory,
so we are lucky,

which means we do not have to be brave.
It is no good having to be brave
all the time. You'll see. I see

those ones who do. In the evenings
they walk their snuffling mutt,
smoke slowly their cigarettes.

Watch the world, child,
it will teach you. See, this is courage—
how he sets his steak-thick hand

to the small of her back,
how she bends and itches the ears
of that lucky, goddumb dog,

the way they breathe and their very breaths—
smoky, full of evening's coming freeze—
seem too big for them to breathe.

# J & W Redemption, Highway 9, North Iowa

In the young year's first burst of crocuses,
                in late summer's hum of gas grills and locusts,
in December's bone-deep freeze—
                the highway ice, the sky ice,
the very mustache hairs—
                in all this, they come,

come bearing such sacks—large and lumpy as a man,
                as two men—these great sacks of tall Coors cans,
of squat Schmidt cans, and box after box
                of mismatched bottles—
Old Crow, Rich & Rare, some generic vodka,
                a longneck or three, the funny beer
some sister's friend down from Minneapolis brought
                and said was good
but wasn't, even those few of frosted glass gone rose
                with the last of the wife's pink wine—

O, they bear it all! On thick backs,
                they bear it. In flannel-shirted arms,
they bear it. Over broad and sagging bellies,
                they bear it. How they suffer it!
Tender the evidence of their actuality,
                their vitality, the very vessels
of their spirit and shook courage,
                the real work of their bacciferous
and fatty bodies—all this of them
                they lay down before her—

this smooth-skinned, slender-fingered one,
                    slim-hipped, small-breasted St. Peter
of receptacle deposits, angel in a Carhartt coat,
                    the redemption gal.


O, what loveliness is hers! is her gloved hands,
                    lifting (as those very hands were surely
lifted once by God and plumbed
                    for His purposes) three-by-three
last season's collectable cammo pattern
                    High Life cans. What generosity is hers!
Who counts—one, two, three, four—
                    the empty liters of Beam
and nary says a word! Who all day
                    with her small, upturned nose
and makeupless-but-plum-anyway lips,
                    breathes the quince of whiskey
and worse. Yes, what grace is given


                    is given. For one day I came and stood in line
with all the others, with my clinking box of bottles,
                    and just as I set them before her,
on that low, slick, sour bench,
                    the man in the back office—
the bald one with the greasy ponytail—
                    stomped out and hollered, *Listen,
you skinny bitch, he's a goddamn nuisance
                    is what he is. I'm taking your goddamn kid home!*
And he did. He jerked the boy
                    out the door, and there was the small sound
of breath leaving the boy, the scream
                    of the door on its hinge,

and there was no other sound.

        Not a one of us, not even the man nearest me,
his forearms the size of pines,

        his steak face jerking at that spit *bitch*—
not a one of us said a word. And I heard

        in that awful silence the pure, sad surprise
of what the final reckoning must hold—

        imagine the long list of transgressions
given, all faithlessness and venality

        laid out on the table, the stink of it
like damp ash or a child's wet sheets,

        and yet from her right hand this deity
pulls anyway her blue rubber glove

        and licks quickly her thumb (again I see
her crooked smile, chipped eye-tooth,

        the way her contralto slid that day from *thanks,*
like a slick tire grabbing gravel)

        and thumbs up for you a check,
for that which you came to redeem.

## With the Kisses of Many

The rain tore the morning
like a shirt, like a shawl, any scrap
we might use to keep the back-raking
weather off our backs. On the sidewalk

not leaves but their rain-bled ghosts.
Then a man with wires
in his eyes, salt-crash
of snails beneath his shoes. Once,

at a funeral for a girl I didn't know,
I carried the broken body
of God. Once, there was a boy
I did know, his shoulders

dimpled with the kisses of many
lit cigarettes. And here, now,
along the busy floodroad's verge,
rain slanting down and down,

a woman waits to cross, her children
so tight to her hip it is impossible
to tell how many there are.

## Today, the Neighbor Girl Wore a Blue Dress, and Her Doll Was Naughty at Tea

So as if there is nothing
else to do

but this—

she
swings it hard against the fence.

# Note to My Unborn Son concerning the Fundamental Project of Democracy

His beard hairs hang straight off his face and, like water around you, his stink of liquor and rancid limes—drab green coat with pockets, jeans an evening shade of blue, scabbed ankle bones because he isn't wearing socks. And now the rainbowed cotton of his shirttail taking sail.

A wind to be reckoned with, that's for sure.

Though otherwise here in north Iowa the cornflower sky opens wide as some good god's eye, an early winter light laves the black oaks, the buckeyes, the flame-headed maples ringing the courthouse, which today is as busy as it ever is, with all the gray-haired couples and mothers toting squealing, red-cheeked babies and shivering college kids in T-shirts and sweatpants and everyone wearing on their collars or over their hearts flag stickers so small all the stars are one smashed star.

Oh, don't forget the dead! Back of the courthouse the three stone slabs etched with the names of neighbors' great-uncles and distant cousins and like children's rhymes the places where they fell: Vicksburg, Big Horn, Belleau Wood, Saipan, Cha La, Fallujah.

And when he finally speaks, you think with his corn kernel teeth and olfaction of rotting fruit he is surely derelict, and you are busy, face bitten in the wind but the rest of you too hot in your winter coat, yet it is election day, and the light an ocean you're under, so you stand and nod and listen.

Back in '72, he is telling you, he rode with his young man's pink lungs and lean legs a bicycle clear across the country and—*Hear me now*, he says, a hand held up between you, so you might study the intricate black craquelure of each knuckle—there was a time in Wyoming, flat tire, ninety lonely miles of two-lane, and surely the light wouldn't last, when along came this old plains woman who didn't speak a lick or snort of English—maybe Austrian or Cossack Russian or something—along she came in a rattletrap pickup and drove him all the way to Laramie and didn't say a word, though he talked the whole time. Even told her about his father. How his father looked at him, his father's hands.

*When she dropped me off,* he says, his rheumy eyes clearing, *she took hold of my face, like this. Then kissed me where I had been talking so much, here, on my mouth.*

# Fishcutter

This morning I sharpened knives,
oiled the blood-leather of my work boots.
You think it's easy? You think it's frozen fillets,

pearly clean and $3.99 a pound? You think you know

the world? This morning I dressed in plastic,
worked a blade up a thousand bellies,
pulled what was inside out.

# Me & Mississippi

On Farish then & ever after, the sun is on my shoulders,
like an early morning rain at first
but mouth hot now,
wet flame all the worse because it's wet, because you ought not
to be so hot swimming through the way
you have to do. Oh, I know I should
know you upside & down, Mississippi,
but I guess all these years again there's nothing so blue
as the true blue of a policeman's blouse,
silent, knife-headed dog lunging, once,
on its leash, & the crowd
giving me not a few stink-eyed looks, & him
acting like everything is A-OK fine,
pulling me along, hustling me down Farish & onto Pearl
& talking supper chops & Donnie Ray & that business
with the new fish pond up near Itta Bena—

he's right pulling me off my feet, & I tell him
stop, I'm going to fall, & he says
don't you right here in the street for anyone & everyone dare—
don't you goddamn dare.
Later, on the TV set,

a high-school boy, a good, lean-looking boy,
slaps her face, smears the ketchup in her hair.
I touched her shoulder, I say,
not to him or anyone but me & Mississippi,

me & the burning, dirty river in me,
me & what I might have been.

# Littlelight

*. . . and this is the crime of which I accuse my country and my countrymen
and for which neither I nor time nor history will ever forgive them, that
they have destroyed and are destroying hundreds of thousands of lives and
do not know it and do not want to know it.*

—James Baldwin

Don't explain the blue Chevy, abandoned
six miles up the gravel of Grapevine Road.

Don't explain the inestimable weight
of snow, of snapping prairie silence,
ice crystals in the vitreous of eyes.

Don't explain those eleven winter-lost days,
infant shoes pulled from a gulch in late May.

When they found what was left of the Littlelights,
I turned my back on the night, even as it squawked
and beat its black wings. When they found

strewn clothes and bones and trace amounts
of meth in the DNA, they didn't find anything.

*—for Teddy, Juliet, and Cole Littlelight*

42

# Prairie Race Relations, Lodge Grass, One Sunday Afternoon

There we were, some dozen of us,
draped across car hoods or asses down in the dust
and backs up against bald tires, maybe shoulder-slouched
into the sunlit bricks of downtown's abandoned false-fronts.
Someone was slapping a beat on a fender, rhyming
*rez life, white wife,* and *knife.* There was a bottle
of Canadian Mist we all took turns tugging on.
One of the girls had stolen a fistful
of her mother's Newports. I don't think
I was yet sixteen. All in all, things were looking good.

Still, it was deep summer on the plains,
and even though my neck and the backs of my hands
had lustered clear to burlap or dry river mud,
they were darker. Driftwood, worked saddle leather.
Most were Crow, some Cheyenne. A few windy storms
of various prairie bloods. The prettiest one
took my hand in hers. Her voice was heavy rez
and hard for me to understand. She must
have made a joke because the others laughed
and looked away. Maybe she was sorry,

maybe she meant every word—
but with the terrifying power of a penitent
or a lover, she knelt on the crumbling sidewalk,
knelt before me and traced the lines
of my still white palm. *Look here,* she said,

her fingers light and warm as wind
against my skin, *you might be Indian
after all. This line says you'll either have to leave
or die.* Thinking it another joke, I turned away.
*I'm serious,* she said, and in the ashy gravel

pulled me to my knees. *You should leave.*

# Like Bread the Light

Down there is the bar ditch. The wild mustard tall as me in places and my hair long as it was then caught up in mustard and a few stray burs and bits of driftwood from whenever the last rain was and riffles and sighs of dried mud and dust when you laid me down on the dirt and gravel and kissed me in the bar ditch.

You were pulling at my T-shirt. The snap of my jeans. My panties. I was thinking I would like you to touch as much of me as needed touching. Which right then was a whole lot. I was thinking but not really thinking. Not like you. In your head the way you always were I wondered if you might up and decide it not a good idea and leave me there. Leave me there in the bar ditch. You didn't. You did one good thing. I can say that. God but all those long days hauling hay in the summer sun had roped our arms and umbered our shoulders and necks and strawed our hair. If we were not lovely there in the dust and mustard of the bar ditch then I am telling you it is all for shit. Your wrists the way a river kinks around a rock. Slope and flower of my own breast. And I was breathless.

My old mother watching TV in the trailer. Peanuts in a can of Coors. Dinner plate of crushed cigarettes. My father in Tacoma or Oklahoma or some other gone-the-fuck-away place. It oughtn't to have been any good between us. Young and kindly and dumb as we were. I guess maybe it wasn't. Maybe my old mother was right about you. But even after. When you had gone and given yourself over to your own fears. Those ones you called dreams. When I decided there was nothing left to do but wreck my stupid self on every mean man I ran up against. Every dry-knuckled, chap-lipped man. Even after.

I tell you this spring the rains came hard and the bar ditch ran like a river and in the culvert a tangle of watersnakes unspooled. I saw one day lifting from the ragweed a heron wide as God. Now I move my hands like this over my hips and feel the wind. Now when I do this with my lips it is the wind I kiss.

I guess I hope a few things for you. A wind to roll in your mouth. On your tongue the iron tang and mud lick of dust. That sometimes you are sad in the middle of the day and go walking along a gravel road and squeeze between your blunt thumb and finger the stems of weeds. I hope you understand that summer we lived on sunlight, gnashed like bread the light.

Would you believe it? If I told you it's still in me? That here at the lip of the ditch I fucking shine?

# III

# Note to My Unborn Son concerning Winter, Grief, & Spring

*It was necessary to hold on to the things that mattered.*
*The dead man mattered, the new life mattered.*

—James Baldwin

As if the hours forgot themselves,
this day there was
no light—
only a lifting of the dark
for another dark.

\*

Oh, I am weary & grieved,
for the good man who was our neighbor

last week laid himself down on his sofa
& nestled up against

his temple the pistol barrel & fired.
Child, the blood

of your birth is yet some months away. Today,
would be better. For I am weary

& grieved, & your mother,
she is heavy, too, with both death & you.

\*

He was alone all winter with his suffering.
We heard he'd died but thought it was his heart.
The bad wind had gone bone cold again.

When his sister came to move his things—
*Help,* she said. *Help. I can't let mother see, can't
let mother see. She's a wreck, she's suffering!*

Inside, I thought I might be sick—on the cushion
a good inch thick, a puddle of his blood. No, I thought,
not this. Not the bad wind gone bone cold again.

*Mother see, mother see,* she kept saying. *Goddamn
couch—we have to haul it out!* We stared at what was left
of him, this evidence—so loud—of silent suffering.

We knew him. We knew him only as a neighbor
but anyway hauled that blood-soaked couch out,
where without sound it suffered the bone-cold wind.

We stood there then & shivered. His sister lit a cigarette.
*I knew,* she said, *but didn't know. I mean, it's hard to know
how deep it goes. Whatever it is. The suffering, I guess.*
The wind slapped & battered at us. The wind. The wind again.

        *

In my dream last night a little boy—
towheaded, ornery,

wouldn't leave me be—
*Get the fuck away from me,* I snarled,

my voice not mine & mine.
*The fuck away from me.* He'd lost his factory job,

our neighbor. I count back now,
realize it was the very day before.

He was on his back step,
having a cigarette. Said he couldn't wait

for spring. From budding branches,
robins fat as fists scatter now & fuss.

I tell myself who knows
what any four walls will do, I tell myself

the boy was no boy
but some errant neuron's ugly stutter.

All kinds of things,
I tell myself.

⁂

What to do? What to do but plant
tomatoes, sweet peppers, the three seeds
of cucumber in a single, crumbling hill? But offer
to the one I love—your mother—my hand
as she rises from the broken earth
we hope will be, some months from now,
abundant? We haven't seen his sister since.
That cold day, as we turned to leave,
she took my hand & squeezed so hard it bruised,
the bruises fading only now—

yellow, green, & faintest blue. Child,
before this goes any further,
know you owe us
nothing. We did this—garden, wish, & grief—
without your consent. You will eat the air
& scream. We will be wrong
to silence you.

# Poem thinning out into prayer

Along the gravel alley,
    oak and tangled shadow,

the grass going blue, now stars,
    gnats    breath of diesel    O god

    of busted wishes
leave me here    a long time here

    in the stinking    dark

# Anyone who has eyes for seeing should see

I will call you god-in-things
for I have no other words for your seven red arms,
your boot-shattered face. The world
your highway eyes, tongue
of green weeds. See? I call you god-in-things—
your morning gap and stretch the steaming spines
of maple and ash outside my window,
funny anus of sunlight. I have no faith.

God-in-things the other day in a magazine
there was a photo of a seven months' infant
filling with earth. His bowels
twisted by your bad hand. His face was not angelic
with suffering. It was vile, and I saw
you, god-in-things—saw you
in the way his lips peeled from his teeth. You see
I have no faith. When I fall

your unclean arms fold around me.

## The Can Picker, 1st & Cowls

I will tell you what it means to have been miles
& be back now in the early afternoon
to the Baptist Church,
my nest of gingko leaves & rags—
it means the early fog rode my right shoulder,
the last stars my left. Means an arrow
of crying geese
when I close my eyes. Means back of the Valu-Mart
a coyote snouting through the night's grease.

Means bootslap, early blister, bootslap.
Means oil slick, diesel stink, tire whine, piston shriek
machining my all-day ear. Means wait
at the light, hole in the heart, piss & rain & puddle—
means, & thank Christ, coffee
at the diner on the highway,
where the waitresses are motherdreams
& mean as angels. You know the bones, the aches
& vapors, the creaks & cracks, the one cold rib
you split all those years ago
slipping on a riverrock that time
fishing with your father. Means your gone father
walks with you. Every gone & going
lover walks with you. The world is whiled away
with the dead & alive & who-knows host
of those you love—

& can you say the same? Can you,
when you come upon me
in my raggy corner beneath the church's gabled roof
picking through my fifty gallon sack of cans—
can you when you come upon me, & I see you
seeing me, & I call hello to you—
can you call hello back to me? Can you see
we have this day on the earth each done
what is ours to do? Can you see
that by grace or happenstance or whatever
you give breath or fire, we are here,
at 1st & Cowls, adored each
by the green hands of gingko leaves?

## Note to My Unborn Son concerning the Peculiarities of Faith

Just skinny girls and boys
but they hold anyway
green-streaked fingers

to the sky, as if even now—
tear gas coming down,
sad-eyed men

owned by some other man
shouting orders,
wrecking precisely machined

clubs against
ordinary necks and knees,
rifles on their backs intricate

and tall as them—as if even now
some god's on duty. Down,
I hunker

down, watch
each video blip and break. Hips
like thinning brooms,

I think. Beautiful
beyond themselves. What a thing—
to believe.

# Caddo River Elegy

*At least 16 people, including some children, were killed Friday*
*after flash floods swept through their remote Arkansas campsites.*
—abcnews.com, June 11, 2010

In the hot dark we lay like fishes—
　　　　　wet & nosing one another at the gills. In my gut
an old bullfrog thwumped.
　　　　　With a whine & haw
a locust sawed at my night heart's
　　　　　moorings. In the earth, I knew, were ancient bones,
on the earth were my new bones.
　　　　　I rolled & nosed my yeasty mother,
rolled & nosed my bleary, beery father.
　　　　　I forgot exactly where I ended,
where the rest began. As if water
　　　　　all around us. As if I were already water,
I slid that night into their nostrils,
　　　　　into the heave & hollow of their lungs—
ran every crook, slew, & swerve of them,
　　　　　by flapping hearts was driven
clean into squinched arterioles. God,
　　　　　I loved their bodies. Back-to-belly in the tent
we lay like fish & breathed the salt
　　　　　rising from each others' skins. What I wouldn't give,
I thought, to never sleep but wake,
　　　　　& into each diminishing minute,
wake again. Yet, as it does, sleep took me,

          though it took me to the day before the night,
to a slow pool of the Caddo River,
          where with leeches I caught three bream,
to that bramble where the blackberries
          bruised & ran with even the lightest finger,
to the slough where I squatted down
          & watched a turtle blow & settle in the mud
until but for his eyes he was mud.
          Baby was sick & the blowflies sticky,
so mother put her in the tent,
          where she slept all day & only squalled
when I leaned kindling sticks
          against a stump & snapped them with my boot.
At dinner we fried the bream
          in peanut grease. Boiled greens with tomatoes
& bones. Not even mother
          waited for a bowl, & spoon after spoon we slurped
ice milk straight from the old crank jug—
          it hurt my teeth it was so cold. Later,
we scrubbed with sand, unlaced our boots,
          lay down like a row of fishes in the tent. As we dreamed
of the good day past, the water came

          & took us & we were killed.
You might think there would be a buoying,
          there was no buoying. Like the bad hand of God,
water slammed us down, pinned us
          to the earth & snapped our every rib. Oh,
how does God or anyone bear day
          & night? I tell you if this world
is a good father's sloping shoulder,
          the stink of river & ripe blackberries. If this world

is a wall of killing water,

         a man reaching into the floodtrees

for the small & tangled bodies—

         then goddamn it, then you best grieve & eat it.

A muddy bank of the Caddo River

         is where I'm dreaming now, where a vole snouts

through my throat, where a tree frog's scream

         fills my heart's dark riffle.

# Encomium, Driving Highway 49 South


Fog this morning. Thick. And loving the thick bodies
of live oaks, the skinny-hipped cypress. The way
                         fog is the world before me,
closes the world behind me.
                         Still I know the river
is there. We move south together, each bend
and turn of ourselves.

   *


Near Midnight, Mississippi, the steep-banked roil
of the Yazoo slows, spreads,
                    hangs like the one time
as a boy I saw my grandmother. Naked. Her belly.

   *


See how cypress reach into swamp water? Into dead leaves?
Into mud? Can you imagine? Mud
           what you love? In this world of six winds mud the one
who holds you? You hold?

   *


I must be lost. The ocean,
             this great-swallowing body, has taken
the highway, the trees, my river. I walk waveblown sand, scrub
                         a grit of it from my eyes.
We know so little. We must believe
in everything. So let us pray:

To grandmothers and rivers,
pray. To thick oaks and any town called *Midnight*,
pray. To sagging, naked bellies, to mud in your hands,
my mouth of sand,
pray. To fog and this morning, from the fog
like dark revelation, the blackbirds rising—
their thousand wings and the one wind a chorus,
an orison that was, I swear, this
sound of waves, pray.

## Note to My Unborn Son concerning the Second Law of Thermodynamics

When we woke, she said, sleepily,
*Let's sleep.* So we did. Just minutes more,
but the earthborn heat between us
was supernal. I lay there

between worlds—
sunlight and the sound of rain rending
the edges of my dream—

and ran my fingers along the ridge of her belly,
where the very muscles are unknitting,

the body dismantling itself
for the other body:
and it was not

making's heat that warmed me then,
but unmaking's

surer fire. With a shudder
I woke into this world
of light and loss—

woke wholly, knowing even for the rain
you will burn us down to ash.

# Absence

For you I drink a cup of wind, taste two fingers of salt.

For you I do not bathe & grease builds back of my ears & tangles my
lank hair, the vagabond whiskers on my nose.

For you pine duff, blueberry, wild mint, a fawn's slender hoof &
fetlock.

For you I chew weeds & rain-rotten sticks, drag my bare feet through
dew-soaked grass.

For you I refuse the advances of the mountain.

For you I curse & stomp rocks, each thwomp & ring winging up shin
& spine, rattling the very jaw socket.

For you I wander open-mouthed under the cloud-shot sky & do not
watch where it is I am going & with a wet pop turn my ankle &
fall & scrape my hands & knees to the wet quick.

For you stump & limp.

For you abrasion, bruised bone, little driblets of blood.

For you six days of sun & seven days of silence, warm water from a
tin cup.

For you I wander out again & step through a scruffy slope of
meadow, the lewd unfurling of ferns, dewy & vaginal field of
purple-flowered moss, & on down to the lake, lilies like scoops
of butter corking on the wind-cut water.

At moonset I wake & rise & piss a great arc out the front door &
leap from the steps & up the hill I run, the lean god of absence
gnashing my devotion, & a fishbelly wind scours my skin & my
eyes leak light & my sick heart judders in its pocket of gristle &
rib, & each winging rib & each slick joint & each juddering leg
bone for you, & for you this road & road dust & lip salt & the
salt-hungry tongue & this breath & breath—

# Note to My Unborn Son concerning Time, Fear, and Impending Fatherhood

Almost ominous,
the corn lifting grain of loam by loam
above the fields,
the sudden russet streaks
ambering the tomatoes. Violent,
is a better word. The inexorable blaze
of becoming.

# The Garage Sale Daze Meditations

i

Look at them, slumped in the corner there.
Ears pounded and mouse-bitten,

ragged legs askew. Rubber lips kissing
cold cement. Even here, among the abandoned,

they are twice forsaken:
the coffee cup, chipped to a wobble,

is ever at hand; the faded sweater
desires shoulders, sure,

but a hanger anyway does the trick;
even that flattened football

fairly whistles with tossed potential.
What is it that goes out of dolls?

They have never been more
than what they are. How is it they now

look less? *Don't look,*
says the mother, left arm crooked

and loaded with a dozen pairs of slacks.
*Honey, if they scare you, just look*

*the other way.* Her little girl knows already
we're only going the one way,

and so takes the measure of these
one-eyed, earless, hacked-bald dolls—

takes a step closer, her own rubber soles
kiss-kissing cold cement.


## ii

On every one
she's put a price tag. Oh, sure,
as old alphabet blocks go

they're good—
this clown's lips still strawberry,
each tree green and tall—

but why is S twenty cents?
And why, Q, are you
a dime less demanding?

Or Mister Victory,
upright V, with your violet ink
and predictable violin,

why do you
deserve not just a dime
but a dozen cents? It doesn't

make any sense. Though maybe
her first husband was a Leon
or a Larry—

and that's why L
is had now for the linty nickel
at the bottom of my pocket.


### iii

*Wayne*, it says, on the back of the upright mirror,
in blue crayon. The woman
at the shoebox till, hair crimped and bleached,
can't be more than twenty-four. I don't hear
a thing from the house. And too,
there are the toys—
yellow dumptruck without a wheel,
box of just-worn baseballs. Those few pairs
of some small boy's patch-kneed jeans. Where,
oh where, can he be? God
of garage sales, of Jefferson Airplane 8-tracks,
of mismatched rose-patterned plates,
of shave-cream bottles shaped like rocket ships
and stilettos red as sour candy, of sixteen neon T-shirts
imploring one and all to *Eat at Jake's,*
of just-a-dollar, three-for-one, you-won't-find-another,
of all things culled from basement closet corners,
of all things wearing a decade's furze of dust,
of all things justly and unjustly
junked—I pray now, here, in this stranger's
strange garage, for this one, whose blue name
is Wayne.

iv

Iowans are easy, all smiles
and apologies, but the nicest set of drawers I've found

belongs to the Italian down the street—
all his eighty years

and ninety-eight pounds given to rage,
rage at whatever idiocy

the new day brings. Today,
I offer thirty. His old face fists,

his two fists like birds shot dead. *You think*
*my things are not so nice? You think*

*I sell this good thing I bought in Omaha*
*with my own money? Bought when I was young, too?*

*When I was man as you? That's what you think?*
*Thirty-two fifty. You haul it out yourself.*


v

It's gotten darker than I hoped. And so,
after fingering for hours
the hidden, homely things of these—
my townsmen and -women—
I'm on my way back home. Before I left,
you said, *Only what's on the list.*
And because I love you, I promised,

69

though right off I think you'll understand
these LPs—look here,
Little Feat's *Dixie Chicken*—
couldn't be passed up. The Jimmy Carter
coffee cup? That may be a stretch—
but it was only fifty cents. And for a buck
I got this charcoal grill shaped like a can of Pabst—
can you believe it? Just a buck! Yes,
I found a rocking chair, changing table, swing,
and bouncing seat. Yes, now we're ready. Yes,
I'm happy as can be. Yes, yes, life is made
of castoff things. God, yes—we need that yellow pail!
It's for him. To carry things in. Whoever he is,
whatever he needs to carry.

## Note to My Unborn Son concerning Canadian Folk Music

Working now around the great bulk of her belly—
that blue-veined globe, blood-thrummed world
of which we know and know so little—
she sets the dimple of the Alvarez on her knee
and with her water-swollen hand frets
a Gordon Lightfoot tune, the one about the rain.
Listen, little fish, I want to know: does omphalos blood ring
with the quiver of sheepgut strings? Do you bow down
and rise up, the lone ocean of you
storm against some placental sand? Is the voice of love
wavery, waterlogged, beyond us always? With her mouth
she sings, sings, *An aching in my heart,*
*my pockets full of sand.*

# IV

# Six Days' Lament

*I think I disagree that there is a quantum leap between living and non-living.*
— George Church, professor of genetics,
Harvard Medical School

So at nineteen he gave his life to God,
           & now—hands slippery as fish, skin
pocked & spotted, beard
           falling, simply falling from his face—
he asks about that girl I knew, the one
           who sat next to me in his section of honors lit,
who when we were both nineteen
           & drinking at some ridiculous college party
fell three stories
           & broke below. I remember

he had us reading then
           *The Grand Inquisitor,* though when I came to see him
at the Jesuit House, we didn't
           speak of it. (*How will you live?*
Aloysha asks. *How will you love them?*
           *With such a hell in your heart and in your head?*)
& neither do we now. Speak,
           that is, of love, this pause,
my pause, falling awkwardly between us.
           *She's good,*

I tell him. *She's in a home,*
           *has a job answering phones*

at a lawyer's office in the afternoon.
          Then takes her pills, sees her movie,
is asleep religiously by seven.
          Like stuck birds at the dirty glass
his old lips flap. *I wouldn't*
               *want,* he says, *to live*
*like that.* & days later just like that


          he is dead, or anyway down far enough
that river road of lotus flowers,
          some dichotomist named him dead
& dead & dead forever. But you see,
          it was happening: years ago, he'd have never
said a thing like that. Or the way
          that day he spoke & closed his cloudy eyes,
then woke & spoke again—about this time
          something else entire. The way even now

she sometimes says my name,
          & in her blue eyes birds take wing—
though a moment later her face
          goes slack, then spastic. It's happening—
for eighty years that brilliant,
          god-wracked man falling into the bounds
of his body: for however many years
          she'll ever have that godblown girl holding
in her trembling, not-quite fist the phone:
          or this one, God, this one I hold,
my six days' child, already
          sloughing off his birthing skin.

# Each Word Holds the World

The sky gray as dishrags, she wore anyway
cutoffs and a pink bikini top, black mascara, inked snake forever
curling up her thigh. As if to gather up some secret sun,
she leaned into the fence. Then slipped

a menthol between her lips. More than once I've seen her
leg her way into a rust-bitten Ford—
one slope-jawed boy or another
draped over the wheel, a sneer for this girl

and all the world—and not even give a look
to her shambling, diabetic grandfather,
fumbling with the screen door, hacking a lung of tire-kicked dust.
That day the apples, too,

were falling. Worm-bitten, bird-pecked—
of a sudden she kicked a fist-sized fruit down the gravel,
and the sound wasn't right, the puff of dust that rose
almost iridescent, a bit of spun light

spilled by such ordinary thoughtlessness
and rot. She saw it too. For she kicked another,
gave a laugh. All week I've been hearing her—creek water,
plucked strings, apple blossoms dropping on the breeze—

and fearing I, too, shamble through some stygian,
sugarless world. So, as now I do, I turn
to you, child, whose fingers daily drink

your mother's face, whose blue walls
still bellow and sing—and say to you
some ordinary thing.

# Complaint with Exhaustion & Amateur Theology

At the trough of each sob
the man believes the child might sniffle off
into sleep—
                yet, always,
                            it rises—
saw-blade wail, lung-ragged roar,
hammering scream that takes
                            & breaks
the night's back. Hours now,
                    &, finally, it is as easy
as opening
            & closing the front door,
as jogging half a block, as slowing
to silence beneath the sickle moon,
his heart's bell
                    unringing. Children cry,
he reasons, & some hour, still—
                        whether or not
anyone is there to listen—
                        & it is not so far
to the edge of town, the shadowed aluminum factory,
that ruined & perfect field of corn. God made the world
out of vanity, & now must listen to every
life-shattering
                lie, hold the feverhand
of every strung-out kid shivering in piss
on a cement floor. The night air lashes

                                        the hollows
of his ears. Until he loses count he counts stars,
& no bell now
              but a rippling, watery light
his heart drifts in the dark.

# Colic

If I have loved, I suppose
it is because I am supposed
to love. Go ahead,
scream at me. I don't know
what I'm doing. For instance: the garden's failing.
Last night I sliced through a tomato's
black, grub-run heart and almost
ate it anyway. It's too much. I mean by that
everything: fireflies humping brightly
in the unmown lawn, another
of cat's dead birds at the front door,
the aluminum plant down the street—weedy breath
and busted windows. How they're packing guns again
in Arizona. The way some kid e-mailed the whole class
his suicide note. What I mean is, why
do we even do this? I don't know but dance
anyway around your ridiculous
blue room, as you throw your too-heavy head again
away from me, little lip-slit a wound,
tear letting slip the heart's scream,
Why did you do this?

(later)


Urge and wrestle of neuron, synaptic sizzle
and fizz, red-faced dream of—of what? Empty breast?
Birth's bone vise? Or before? Say that watery dawn,
in which some screaming cell split, tore itself in trembling two

and two and two? I have rent myself as well.
Here in the half-dark, I am done
and undone: the very space between your breaths
shivers, shatters me. Vast as God
and sadder, I fall to my knees, praise
whatever terror this is that takes and twists
your fisted, moon-slick face. Go ahead,
scream at me. Scream and breathe, and I will know
you are alive, as I am.

# Missouri River

In the night he considers distance, those glassy miles of highway
   unrolling through the hours.
In the night he considers hours, dawn's cooling coffee & fading radio
   news, that bad hamburger in Luverne, the long & lengthening
   prairie shadows.
In the night he considers the slanted light of late afternoon, the way
   it lay in gilt striations on the river, which was wide & dark &
   warm.
In the night he considers rivers, the concurrence of limestone seep
   & silty delta & the sinuous, insisting commerce between them.
In the night he considers sand & red-flecked silt, the unblemished
   skin of driftwood.
In the night he considers skin, its nature & function, worries at the
   way the child has no regard for the departure of skin & sand,
   sand & water, the red water of her body's opening.
In the night he considers how as the dark came down she turned to
   him, her skin still flushed, sheen of sweat on her lips, & beside
   them in the tent the child—little knuckling of their own bone
   & flesh & coupling breath—slept.
In the night he breathes & cannot sleep.
In the night he breathes & cannot sleep yet does not rise because he
   does not wish to wake them.
And so, in the night, he blinks & breathes & considers space & time
   & the arrant prairie dark about him, the far milk spots of
   stars, rain owls easing their talons around the spines of voles
   & sparrows, & he thinks too—his heart beginning to knock
   in its bone pocket, blood thrumming in his ear—of these
   stars, & mile after grassy mile of this river, & then this river, &
   they were not the same river, like the particular hours of the
   day before the night came down & the ordinary & immense

& terrifying joy that became him in those white, glassy, gone
hours.

In the night, finally, he risks rolling over—susurrus of fleece & thin
cotton & skin—to look with night-shot eyes at the woman, &
beyond her the child, to consider again the long light of late
afternoon, the way it lay on the skin of the river & her bare
neck & shoulders, the child lifting to his lips two hands of sand
& water.

# A Story We Might Follow

Snow-suit zipped and buckled,
hat strapped beneath his button chin,

I set my son down a moment,
to strap on my snowshoes—

and stove-legged, star-armed
he toddles off after a turning leaf,

down the road that's now a sunblown
wing of ice. When I scoop him

into his pack, he goes stony,
little mouth a nut until I lift him

onto my shoulders, into the sky.
We shoe up and slip down drifts,

wend our slow way through oak
and heavy-headed sumac,

now a tight stand of leaning trees—
smooth-barked, pale as apricots—

whose names I do not know.
I lecture anyway on woodrat voles

and wrist-thin rabbit holes,
this byzantine busyness of claw

nock and hoof pock in the blue
and faultless snow. As cold

as these last nights have been—
every track is purposeful, I know,

but today they seem even more so:
letterings or glyphs, a story

we might follow to some ancient,
quaking, blood-warm source—

or would it be conclusion?
A purling wind rattles sticks,

salt and meltwater at my lips.
It is time to kneel and shrive—

I cannot parse the stories. The hour
might be mine, it might be yours,

it might in the coming cavalcade
of griefs slip like a snowmelt wind

from each of us. I rise, we rise,
and walk another mile, rustle up

a great barred owl, watch carp
dart beneath the river's lace of ice.

# Complaint with Parking Lot Vegetable Stand & Child's Cry

& so because sunlight
                    because leaf litter floodwater hot loam
& other frankly sexual things
                    because each day a break-of-day rain
weds this ripe earth & every mean seed upon it
                    because all summer then
from any old blacktop crack or bar ditch thin unwanted stalks rise
& rise cleanly
                    like country boys fated to war or manufactory or worse
the absence of either
                    so this evening streaks of fresh tar rainbow
the faded strip mall parking lot
                    scatter the tatty light
& like rusty tongues the tailgates of these pickups loll & proffer
the vegetal sacraments of swine-heart tomatoes
                    flame-shaped peppers
knurled kohlrabi tasting I know faintly & strangely of the sea
& so there is an ocean in my mouth
                    when the child cries & my blood's tide
lifts for I am sure that cry is my child's cry my child my own child
sweet deceiving christ
                    where is my child
                    hugging the pumpkins
I find him hugging the pumpkins & scoop him up & on my hip again
he is whole & whole & so
                    these saw-blade cries still whanging

my ears are those of some other's child not my child my child
reaching now for the streaky sheen of the lot's new tar
                                        for the blue-dark
eggplant I was so recently appraising & simply dropped
                                it is a shame & I am ashamed
at the way my blood falls like warm rain back to me & I squat down
& heft the fruit that will feed our flesh & no other
                                & wish the light like this & the rain
& the broken earth abundant
                        & all of us like my son & me unworthy & rising

# Complaint with Drought and Economic Downturn

Mock orange gone rusty and slack,
the hard, weedy pinks of hollyhocks—

oh, what might drink this dry light
and shine? In a season of such want

it seems nearly indecent, my child's brimful
laugh, her delight in the alley's sunblown gravel.

The real work is to remain human:
to remember that like the ashy stone

she fists and studies, then turns to offer,
she is only one among the others—

oh, I know, yet fall still to my knees,
make of my hands a cup. This rock I receive

as if her touch were alchemic, as if
her choosing and her giving are enough.

# Arguing with James Baldwin the Day after the Reelection of Barack Obama

*It has been vivid to me for many years that what we call a race problem*
*here is not a race problem at all: to keep calling it that is a way of avoiding*
*the problem. The problem is rooted in the question of how one treats one's*
*flesh and blood, especially one's children.*

—James Baldwin

On her deathbed your grandmother,
a former slave, hands you a tin box, which you open
to find not sweets, as she thought and you expected,
but needles and thread—

and how old were you then?
I can't take it. Not today. And so close

your busted, back-of-the-stacks book,
and with a hangover big
as the half-abandoned Midwestern burg
I wander, in the early winter light

I blink and wonder. See, I'm trying not
to feel like a dumb sucker, trying to believe
this mess we're in is getting better. Plain as you
once were, or me,

or any color of any boy in these United States,
my son has just turned three,

and this yes, or rather
this hoped-for-but-unexpected yes again, this re-election—
this has got to be something,

right? The highways are crumbling,
the war's still on,

but come on?

\*

It's cold out,
every other storefront empty. I walk by
and think there's something there,

though it's only ever
my reflection. At least these streets

know me. These last six months of knowing
what to do, of walking this way up,
and that way down, of knocking on door after door,
listening and explaining and registering to vote—

I wish the work was done,
wish I didn't know
who's about to lose their home,
who's still furloughed at the plant, which door
leads to a sick child's
dark room. I'd like to say a thing

to smash glass, wreck bricks,
rearrange the light—

the way to a pillow of ash I've laid my flaming head
ever since I was fourteen and first read your book
about fire. Listen,
I'm a liar.

*

The day before the election
I took the morning off,
hiked instead with my son down to the slough,
and there,

along the abandoned railroad berm,
among rocks and weeds
and bits of trash,
found a bone-brittle milkweed.
Like penitents

we knelt before it.
Frost-shattered, the husk gave easily,
and even for the cold
we shed our gloves to hold
those velvet seeds, white and dark
as prayers in the small cup of my son's hands.

Until a wind lifted the sudden thousand of them,
lifted them to stitch and mend
the sky's gray rags,
those needled threads of light—

we were silent,
absolutely winter still,

and when finally we unbent our knees,
rose from the frayed and oil-stained earth—

you're goddamn right I promised him,
swore wherever they fell,

they'd root and grow.

# The Spirit Entering as Midnight Wind

When you woke and knew the world was wrong.
When you slid from darkling quilts, the gone

heat of her like a snuffed flame. When you found
the backdoor wide and wind-held as a dead man's mouth,

rain slicking the shadowed linoleum. When into the wind
you reached and grasped the latch but waited, as if bidden,

I was the wind passing over you, that cold insistence
inhabiting every dustful corner, those wilting cactus

blossoms, the woman, the child, the other child.
Oh, my child, you knew me from time and time

before. When you were hungry, I was water.
When you were thirsty, I was watery

ham and beans, a plateful. When you, the happy fool,
ran laughing through the scutch grass and up the dune,

you later poured the sand of me from your shoes.
Driving those cypress-dark Delta roads, I was the blues.

I was every last cigarette, every ill and easeless sleep.
I was the dry sheen of light on your dead father's cheek.

When in the emergency room you held your son's fever-
hand, I was the black, abyssal lake filling you, eating

the light. I will never leave you. Not when you close
the door and sop the rain-wet floor, not when you climb

the stairs—cloth-black window, creaks like broken bones—
not when you crouch down and listen for each small one's

steady whir and sigh. No, not even then. For I am the wind
at both gates of the mouth, and I love you, like the wind.

# Wish

From the great meaty boils of wintering burrows
        rattlers stir, shudder, & unspool. Stunned blind
they slip & essingly spill
    down yellow hills, forked tongues
        tasting the gravel road's good heat—
& there, on blue quartz, on schist,
    on the cat's eyes of agates & the rocked remains
        of ancient, oceanic brethren, they coil
into thick, rippling rings, wedge heads
    roosting on the oozeful thrones of snakebellies.
        A whole road of them. Curled here,
curled there, waiting for the blood
    to hiss & rise, the body's whip to willingly
        unloop & lick a strike. They wait & praise
the face of the sun, the white fact of it
    like some child's warm, enormous,
        still-good god. Oh, I'd drive like the devil,
fast & swervy, popping snakes
    beneath my tires. I could feel each small thump
        thwunk up through my spine—
in the rearview then a dusty ribbon
    of red-pocked road. It was as easy
        as a wish, a prayer. The way—
hands on the black wheel, foot mashed
    to the rust-bitten floorboard—I prayed the sky
        might stumble, the rain fall, & the river fill

to the goddamn brim. That my mother
     might love the living like she did the dead. Oh,
          all that was a long time ago, & I have prayed
those wishes down. Today, I hold
     my children close, as we kneel in lashings
          of rusty grass, watch a quick, dappled snake
slip into this other river.

# Ragged Point Road

*Doty, if I confess I do not love you*
*Will you let me alone? I burn for my own lies.*
                    —James Wright, from "At the Executed Murderer's Grave"


Why in the night do boys
                    drive the dirt skulls of hills?
Why do boys slam doors, kick rocks, jam hands

in torn jacket pockets—
                    root for the nothing they know is there?
Why like wingless, sublunary moths do boys gather

in rig-light? In the hard, snapping light
                    of the lone wellhammer rising
to fall, still pulling at the earth's dark sustenance?

Why through heartache, disarray,
                    the grief of cigarettes,
do boys wear the faces of stones? Why do boys wish to be

and be other than stones? Why do boys
                    see one beautiful thing and try forever
to forget?

        *

He swings his leg out before him,
                    tips the off-kilter square of his torso

over that fulcrum,
        and with his good leg catches himself

on the other side.
      That spatter of pits across his right cheek?

A time-lapse relief map
       of dumbshit moments

and hard-luck months. Of course,
        the crumbling stone of his chin,

shoulders hunched
     against the bad wind even now

bearing down. Yet for his Pearl Jam T-shirt,
        that bit of boyishness

around his eyes, I'm betting
     he's not far north of thirty. Iraq, then?

Methamphetamine? Some of both?
       I run along the cross sidewalk,

our perpendicular paths soon to intersect—
        in time, at least—

one of his hitching steps falling, perhaps,
     into the sure ghost of my own. Does he dream

of running? Of being a boy again?
        Scrambling up the bank

from the brown river and running?
               Or was there never a season

without wounds? Was entry into whichever
                         broken world he was handed

the first and deepest harm? Am I,
                 thirty-five and mostly whole,

forgetting myself? Anyway, I am running
                      when I glance at him

and turn away.

     *

*What he will do,*
*he decides, is take her all the way out*
*to where the road forgets itself*
*and is grass.*

*So he fires his old man's GMC*
*and drives north. First,*
*the Brewer place,*
*nothing but windfall boards now,*
*some absentee rancher's ornamental longhorns*
*shitting even in what he knows*
*were the bedrooms. He wonders—*

*and why has he never thought of this before?—*
*why after the bank sale and all these years of ruin*
*is it still called the Brewer place.*
*Though as he wonders*

*he hears his father growl,* Never-you-
goddamn-mind-about-that. *So he doesn't,*
*studies the river instead—*
*not yet bone dry, but close. Then rising*
*beneath his wheels, carrying him*
*that much closer to the dark, the long sweep*
*of the bunchgrass hills, the fishmouths of stars*
*dimpling the black water.*

*He begins to speak to her—*
*of the dry taste of grass on the air,*
*of bats swerving for mosquitos*
*in creek willows and chokecherries,*
*of the way, he is sure,*
*the first steel guitar was strung and tuned*
*to the clatter of tires on a gravel road,*
*a good gravel road like this, windows down*
*and the night pouring in.*

*He tells her of all*
*the many beautiful things he sees,*
*of the heaviness of each on his heart. He reaches*
*for her, as he used to, forgetting*

*she is bound with twine*
*and wrapped in a sheet in the pickup bed.*

    \*

*Above a dry creek,*
*beneath a tangle of chokecherries,*
*the night by the minute*
*blackening,*

*he digs. It takes a long time.*
*The shovel slips—*
*splinters in the quick of his hands.*
*And he is often sick. He wretches*
*until there is nothing*
*left, nothing but the milky spill*
*of moonlight on his boots. Deep within himself*

*he can feel each cleft and wing,*
*each grinding of one bone*
*against another,*
*as if here in the night*
*they would rip themselves*
*from the binding muscle,*
*the prison of the skin,*
*and he would be on the earth*
*as he has on the inside*
*always been—*

*he would be two things,*
*two sad, bewildered selves.*

    \*

I was myself,
        and some other self,

some boy brave and up from the black river
            soundless, stepping in the moony night

from shadow to sage
        shadow. Yes, I was the boy

who held in his hard hands
a carton of eggs,

who was ready to haul off
and throw, who didn't even need to throw

because he was sure of her love,
or some love, or didn't give a goddamn

about love. Yet I was myself as well—
fifteen and fatherless, bespectacled, skinny—

an egg sitting like a promise in my palm,
like a wish for flight, for unburdening

and broken rest, for that beautiful cowgirl
to wing her head around

and for once look at me. And which boy
crouches now through the bar ditch? Which boy

falls to his knees behind her mother's Buick,
gulps at the chill, riverine air

as if drowning? Which boy spins
and throws at her window

but misses every time?
And do both boys weep with me

when I fumble the last egg
and it splatters between my stupid feet?

Or this morning, which angry boy am I
        this morning, when we find a half-dozen eggs splattered

down the length of our car? This morning,
        when my son asks, *Who did this, Daddy?*

and *Why?* This light-shot morning
        when I say, *Probably a bunch of boys*

and *Because they are boys.*
        Like certain kinds of rain

the light this morning
        when he claims, though his voice rises

into a question, *But I am a boy?*

        *

*He lays her down,*
*packs the cool earth over her.*
*As if they might root again and grow,*
*he plants cracked grass stems*
*and broken chokecherry branches*
*in the broken ground. Then rises.*

*He is still a long time,*
*still and silent*
*the better part of an hour, and then he remembers*
*that night in the bar, before whiskey slid*
*like a curtain across his eyes,*
*some scrawny roustabout rattling on*
*about oil work in Wyoming.*

*It wouldn't be horseback work,*
*but with the old man losing the homeplace,*
*he's had to take what he can get.*

*Hours down the road, stars*
*blurring, river losing itself*
*in another river, he forgets again,*

*asks if she'd like to stop,*
*watch bats wheel above the trees.*

\*

This is not an apology.

                      This is trying not to turn away.

This is remembering

            we are who we love,

and how fiercely (and who else

          can we be? I wonder,

as I march into his room

         for some trivial deed I have deemed wrong,

my shame-faced son—

             for if I did not love him

with a blood-love hot enough

         to reprimand, to punish, to lose

and gain each day
      my good self, who, indeed,

would I be?), and so—

           say it—

we must not have been so different,
          that terrible boy and I.

We both loved her.

   *

So I tell myself another story—
         the one about the Meredith woman
who'd years ago lost her mind. How in the rain she ran

along the river
      and then cut north at Ragged Point—
some bit of blood-memory

         carrying her home.
How when she knocked,
and my mother opened the door,

       she wrapped her wet arms
around us all. Said, *I've missed you so.*
She hadn't lived there in forty years.

        My father'd bought the place
from that woman's hard-luck son, and then my father's luck
ran out as well.

On her naked, bony shoulders
my just-widowed mother hung a towel, then called the sheriff.
But tell the rest as well,

the part that needs telling—
how she walks barefoot the river's rain-slick bank,
how the wind takes and tatters her night dress,

how lightning
illumes the shovel of her hips,
how stick-thin and ninety-three her shadow

tops the cottonwoods—
how you never saw her there
but all these sad and happy years later

you see her there—
rain-ravished, thunder-headed, striding
muddy miles and miles.

## "Where Was I before I Was Born?"

With me, though differently—
early light slanting through cypress
and your mother calling, softly,
from the warm, dark room I left
for a glass of water.

Or before, when the beautiful idiot
who was my one burning friend slipped
from the bridge's lip and fell through starlight,
you were the sharp, glassy shards
of light in my eyes.

Or when the man I never knew
who would be my father drove all night
through the prairie dark, his blood howling
for everything and nothing—remember,
he did not know how any of this would go.

With your grandmother, then,
wandering the fields, lowering herself
to the earth, though water-swollen and awkward
as she was it was all she could do to touch and not tear
the small, green hands of wheat.

The long way up from Oklahoma
you rode your great-grandfather's right shoulder.
He was sixteen, wild and tired, and you were the one

dipper of rinse water he was allowed
come nightfall.

The year after, when he swung his two fists
at his own father's drunken face, you
were all the many bones, the bruises rising
beneath both skins. You, the boiling blood. You,
the breath funneling in and out. You,

the mad, hard hearts—
every muscle and sinew, you—
I'm telling you there was a world before
and there will be a world after, and they are the same
and only world, and I turn now and bow

to everything that breaks my heart—
which is where you were, that place
hope lives, in the breaking.

V

# Eight Letters of Explanation, Acknowledgment, & Apology on the Occasion of My Son's First Birthday

Brother,
I see a field. In the long-shadowed time
of evening on the plains, I see you kneeling in the dust,
thin shoulders bent, empty hands
in the humming air before you—
for before you is the tiny & impossible cactus flower,
whose blossom cannot be plucked & held,
cannot be broken in our boys' hands. So I do not
care. I stride like I think a man strides
away from you, my shadow long & lean, like a man's.
Brother, I see a field, the grass bending in a low wind—
one boy given to beautiful things, the other
to his shadow.

Cousin Amy,
It's a good thing you lived in California. Otherwise,
I couldn't have stood it. City girl, I'd never
seen a thing like you: painted toes & pouting lips,
white shorts & white thighs—I thought
I might die. Truly, in that week after the funeral
I wandered into walls, thrashed in my sheets
each hot night, & when you stepped
from the bathroom wrapped in a towel—
your steam-flushed skin, damp hair stuck to your neck—
I spilt soggy cereal flakes all down the front of my shirt.
You were there because your father's brother
died. I was still alive.

Mother,
Thank Christ the saint you gave me saw visions:
angels, demons, kings: on the cold linoleum
of St. Joseph Our Perpetual Guardian
I knelt beside you, like you—lips kissing thumbs,
eyes tight with tears—& prayed
for my own visions: Who plots against us?
Which angel's sword will save us? Why this dust?
& meant by *us*, big sister, me, & little brother: we three
of bowl-cut hair & thrift-store jeans, thrice-caught
church yawn & arpeggio of sleepy amens, little ellipsis
of blond heads bowed like yours: we three small ones
without a father, father, father.

Boy Down the Road,
Remember when in the night your father called again
& again for some goddamn artillery,
for some of that old-fashioned, fuck-all artillery—
& zipped tight into our sleeping bags in the next room,
we giggled? When down at the river your twin sister—
all elbows, knees, & teeth—told us not to worry
about the dollar she'd do it anyway,
& then slipped out of her bathing suit, & I looked
at you, & you were looking, so I looked too?
When your mother slapped your face
& down the rot-wood steps that led up to your trailer,
you fell—your mouth a blood flower—
& together we ran, your mother still yelling,
for my house? Remember? I do. & I hear now
you have left a wife & kids in that same trailer & run
instead circles around the stone streets of Sadr City.
I'm telling you I remember.

Sister,
I'm still angry you chased me with a toad,
called my Lego castle cute. But what I want to know is,
who said you could open the throttle
on the dirt bike & race down the lip of the ditch?
Who said you could make an A in calculus?
I don't know where you heard all that crap,
but the boys were pretty clear with me:
I wasn't supposed to answer any questions in class,
& I couldn't stay in the library at lunch.
After they started calling me book-fucker,
I listened. I guess I don't know how you did it—
were who you were, I mean.

Grandfather,
It's a good thing you lived long enough
to go bald, to slump in the shoulders,
to lay your head back on a greasy pillow after lunch
& be taken by sleep, bidden or not. I'm so happy
I watched you die, that you weren't just alive,
then dead, for too often I will see the blue glow
of the screen, & the suited man's grim mouth move,
& the smoke & the bodies & the wrecked
faces are there, & then not there, & I do not know
how to be brave about any of this. Like you
on that yellowing bed, your naked legs curled
against your chest's collapse.

Lover,
Sometimes wind runs like water
through the rusty ash trees. It was like that yesterday,
when I looked up from the dishes & saw you

bending to your tomato vines. O,
I'm a dirty heretic. *Why me? Why anyone? And when—*
I ask of that impossibly-blue, sun-cut sky—
*when will that glad, fickle bastard happiness flee?* You see,
something in me will not be quiet. I am sorry
about this. Though sometimes I wake in the night,
hand on your moonlit hip,
& I am finally silent & twice heretic
in that praiseful silence.

This One I Call My Son,
I am considering the singular possessive pronoun,
or rather: reconsidering. In my thirty-odd years
I have used it willy-nilly, though nothing
seems now mine. Not even the years—
lake water running the skin of some lost friend,
smoke breathed out into the night. Not even you, child.
With your sky-wide eyes & snaggle-toothed grin,
your love of mud & river grass,
your fearlessness, already you are beyond me,
you grieve & shatter me. After hotcakes & goat's milk,
we loaf & lie about, page through a book of rhymes
& pictures, now roll & tickle, breast
to bare breast—& for a moment here they are,
knocking against one another,
these fugitive hearts.